UNDERCOVER STORY

THE HIDDEN STORY OF
DRUGS

Karen Latchana Kenney

rosen publishing's
rosen
central

New York

Published in 2014 by The Rosen Publishing Group, Inc.
29 East 21st Street
New York, NY 10010

First Edition

Produced for Rosen by Calcium Creative Ltd.
Editor for Calcium Creative Ltd.: Sarah Eason and Ronne Randall
Designer: Keith Williams

Photo credits: Cover: Shutterstock: Elena Rostunova. Inside: Dreamstime: Alexraths 16, Andreblais 37, Barsik 14, B-d-s 26, Bdingman 36, CandyBox 12, Dndavis 17, Elenathewise 27, Karinabak 29, Littleny 30, Luckybusiness 34, Margaretwallace 28, Micro10x 7, Monkeybusinessimages 20, Oguzaral 18, Palangsi 23, Poco_bw 19, Ronstik 22, Sepavo 8, Triocean 4, Twoellis 6, William87 1, 25, Wizzard 11, Yuri_arcurs 5, 10; Shutterstock: Avava 44, Diego Cervo 35, Goodluz 39, Martin Novak 32, Santibhavank P 42, Spirit of america 43, Wavebreakmedia 40.

Library of Congress Cataloging-in-Publication Data

Kenney, Karen Latchana.
The hidden story of drugs/Karen Kenney.—First Edition.
    pages cm. — (Undercover story)
Audience: Grade 5-8.
Includes bibliographical references and index.
ISBN 978-1-4777-2803-1 (library binding)
1. Drug abuse—Juvenile literature. 2. Drugs of abuse—Juvenile literature. 3. Teenagers—Drug use—Juvenile literature. 4. Psychotropic drugs—Juvenile literature I. Title.
RC564.3.K46 2014
362.29—dc23

2013021950

Manufactured in the United States of America

CPSIA Compliance Information: #W14YA: For further information, contact Rosen Publishing, New York, New York, at 1-800-237-9932.

CONTENTS

THE TRUTH ABOUT DRUGS

Almost everybody uses some form of drug. Sometimes people want to feel different. They might have a headache or a cold. They might feel emotions they want to change, such as sadness or anxiety. And they might even be bored or feel left out. Drugs can make people feel different. They might be helpful, such as when asthma drugs help a person to breathe. However, drugs can also have really bad effects, such as when a man falls asleep and crashes a car while under the influence of heroin.

Drugs are substances that affect how a person's body works. Once drugs get into a person's body, they go to the brain. This affects the brain's messages to the body. If a person feels pain, a drug can stop the brain's signal to feel pain in that part of the body. That is why a person can feel different after taking drugs.

DIFFERENT KINDS OF DRUGS

There are all kinds of drugs, both legal and illegal. Some legal drugs are used often and are fairly harmless, such as aspirin and caffeine. Alcohol and tobacco are drugs. Legal drugs can be bought at a store or pharmacy.

An inhaler contains a drug that helps someone with asthma breathe better.

Caffeine is a fairly harmless drug that is used daily by many people.

A doctor can also prescribe legal drugs to a patient. Illegal drugs are drugs that the law does not allow people to possess. They are often highly addictive and damaging to a person's mind and body. Heroin and methamphetamine, or meth, are two illegal drugs.

Drug use can easily turn into abuse. And both legal and illegal drugs can be harmful. Drug abuse can ruin the lives of users and their friends and family.

It can cause harm to a person's body and take control of their mind. Drug use also supports an illegal drug supply industry—one that involves criminals and gangs.

This book examines what drugs are, what they can do, and how people can get help. From first use to addiction, drugs affect not only users, but also friends, family, and society.

CHAPTER ONE

DRUG ABUSE

Josh was a pretty average teen. He came from a middle-class family that was very caring and loving. His family moved around a lot, because his father was in the Marine Corps. Josh had a great childhood, though.

Prescription pills can have dangerous effects if misused or combined with other drugs.

In high school, things started to change for Josh. He was shy and had a hard time making friends. He felt left out and distant. Then Josh met an older group of friends. He started skipping school to hang out with them. He began smoking pot and drinking. Soon he was taking acid, mushrooms, and even cocaine. He didn't seem shy anymore and people wanted to hang out with him.

BREAKING NEWS

>> For some teens, drug use leads to prescription abuse. That is when someone takes a medication that has not been prescribed to that person. Every day around 2,000 teens abuse prescription drugs for the first time.

The drugs soon started taking control of Josh's life. He stole money from his parents. He lost weight and had bloody noses from snorting drugs. His addiction later led to some very hard drugs, including heroin and prescription pills. What started out as a small habit had become a life that revolved around getting and using drugs.

A COMMON STORY

Josh's story is not that unusual among drug users. Casual drug use can quickly lead to addiction—from pot all the way to heroin. And drug addiction not only hurts the user, but it can also hurt friends and family. Besides being harmful to the body, drug use is illegal. Drug users risk their health and break the law to get high.

Many people abuse prescription pills, sometimes stealing them from the medicine cabinets of others.

Prescription pills can be easy to find, too. Most teens obtain or steal them from friends or family. According to the most recent Monitoring the Future survey, prescription pills and over-the-counter drugs were the fifth most abused drugs by twelfth-grade students.

THE EFFECTS OF DRUGS

Different types of drugs have different effects. Some seem to give people more energy, while others slow people down. And some are more harmful than other drugs. Some of the most harmful drugs include heroin and cocaine. Let's take a look at the different types of drugs and their effects:

Marijuana slows down the brain, while certain pills speed up the brain.

Depressants: These drugs slow down brain activity. They can make a person feel relaxed, sleepy, or uncoordinated. Some depressants include alcohol, inhalants, heroin, and marijuana.

Hallucinogens: These drugs change what a person sees or hears. They can make a person see something that isn't there or hear different sounds that do not exist. LSD and Special K (ketamine) are hallucinogens.

Opioids: These drugs are pain relievers. Some highly abused opioids are the prescription drugs OxyContin and Vicodin.

Stimulants: A stimulant increases brain activity. Users feel that they have more energy and confidence. The caffeine in coffee is a mild stimulant. Cocaine and methamphetamine are much stronger stimulants.

Synthetics: These chemically made drugs mimic marijuana, cocaine, and methamphetamine. The drugs are sold in stores, but labeled for use in the bath or as incense. Users have no idea what chemicals are in the mixtures, making them very dangerous. Some synthetic drugs include bath salts and spice. Because most are not yet illegal, synthetics are widely abused.

HITTING THE HEADLINES

BATH SALTS

This drug is cheap and easy to find, but it has really scary side effects. It's sometimes called the Zombie drug because it can make users violently attack other people. Some of its harmful effects include paranoia, hallucinations, and extreme anger. Long-term effects include liver and kidney failure and mental illness or death. The problem of this particular drug use is growing, too. According to the American Association of Poison Control Centers, the number of phone calls to U.S. call centers about bath salts increased from 304 in 2010 to 6,138 in 2011.

Many drugs at first make a person feel really good. They give the user feelings of confidence, energy, or relaxation. After a while the drug wears off and the user "comes down." However, the user remembers the good feelings experienced when he or she first took the drug, and wants to try that drug or other drugs again.

Taking drugs becomes a social thing. Users feel like they need the drugs to have fun at parties. Other people might be using drugs at parties too. They use together. Friendships form around drug use, but they are not healthy relationships.

Some people first try drugs at parties, thinking they'll have more fun.

BREAKING NEWS

>> According to the most recent Monitoring the Future survey, use of certain illegal drugs by middle and high school students is rising or not declining in the United States. Daily marijuana use increased from 2010 to 2012.

HOW DRUG ADDICTION STARTS

At first, using drugs is voluntary. A person might just use small amounts at parties on the weekends. Then tolerance kicks in. Over time the brain gets used to a certain level of drugs. They no longer produce the same high. The user has to take larger doses of the drug to produce those good feelings. That person starts using more often than he or she once did. And coming off the drugs gets harder and harder. The user feels depressed, tired, and lifeless.

Even the ritual of using the tools needed to take illegal drugs can become addictive.

Someone has become dependent on a drug when he or she needs it just to feel normal. The user now takes drugs every day, feeling an overwhelming need for the drug. The user doesn't care about the consequences of using and finds any way to get the drug, even if it means stealing or lying. This is drug addiction.

The survey found that one in fifteen high school seniors used marijuana daily or almost daily. Synthetic marijuana use stayed at a little above 11 percent for twelfth graders from 2011 to 2012.

CHAPTER TWO

TEENS AND DRUGS

Mindy was on the school swim team and liked her French and art classes in high school. She was not into drugs, but her boyfriend was. "I didn't drink, smoke pot, or anything," she said.

Not even schools are safe from drugs and drug use.

Her boyfriend used heroin. Soon Mindy was using it too. She started once every few weeks. Then she had to use every day. She stole money from her parents and lied about her addiction. Finally, she broke down and told her parents. She tried to quit but couldn't— by now Mindy was hooked.

HITTING THE HEADLINES

HIGH SCHOOL DRUGS

A recent CASAColumbia survey found that many American teens are taking drugs during the school day. Here are the results:

- 86 percent: Knew classmates who had taken drugs, drank, or smoked during classes.

- Almost 50 percent: Knew someone who sold drugs at their school.

- 52 percent: Knew a place on or near the school where teens went to get high during school hours.

- 36 percent: Thought it was easy to use drugs at school without getting caught.

For her three-day senior retreat, Mindy and a friend brought drugs and needles. The school's staff found out and called Mindy's parents. They came and took her home. And just two days before she was supposed to graduate, Mindy was expelled. Mindy used heroin, but that is just one kind of drug that teens abuse.

THE MARIJUANA PROBLEM

Marijuana is the most commonly abused drug by teens in high school. It is often easily obtained, and its effects are not as long lasting as those of other drugs. And the problem is growing, especially with prescription pills, synthetic marijuana, and marijuana.

Being a teen can be difficult. Bodies are changing. Hormones can cause emotional ups and downs. And social groups are growing and changing too. It's hard to know how to act, make friends, and fit in. Teens can feel extremely insecure and alone.

Unhappy teens may try drugs to hide their problems.

This is the time when many people start experimenting with drugs. The average age teens first use of marijuana is at the age of 14. Some stop soon after they try a drug. However, others continue using into adulthood, trying harder drugs over time. This is what leads to addiction.

REASONS FOR USING DRUGS

Teens start using drugs for many different reasons. They try drugs to fit in with a group of peers. They feel more social when using and think drugs will make them popular. Some think drugs make them better students or athletes. They use drugs to concentrate better while they study. Some drugs help athletes build very large muscles or run longer than others. Some have terrible problems they want to block out, such as sexual or emotional abuse. Drugs make them feel numb and help them forget. Others just want to rebel or even get attention.

A history of drug use in a family can also be a reason teens start using. They follow a pattern set by their parents or siblings. Watching their family use drugs makes it seem like a normal thing to do. Children learn to cope with their issues by using drugs. Some teens have depression or other mental health issues. They believe drugs help them overcome those problems. The reality is that drugs do not solve problems. Once the drugs wear off, those same problems are still there.

HITTING THE HEADLINES
DIGITAL PEER PRESSURE

Online social networks add to the peer pressure exerted on teens. In a recent CASAColumbia survey, 75 percent of teens said that seeing photographs of teens doing drugs on Facebook, MySpace, or other social networking sites made them want to try drugs.

Drugs are not just bought in drug deals anymore. They're found at parties and other social situations with friends. They're found in medicine cabinets at the homes of friends and neighbors and bought online. Synthetics are still legal to buy in stores. And drugs are also found in schools. It's not too hard for teens to find drugs if they really want to. Teen access to illegal drugs is widespread.

DRUGS IN SCHOOL

Schools are one of the easiest places for teens to find drugs. A recent survey found that nearly 91 percent of the students knew someone at school who sold marijuana. The numbers were smaller for other drugs. Around 24 percent knew someone who sold prescription drugs. And 9 percent knew someone who sold cocaine.

Teens may fake symptoms to get drug prescriptions for illnesses they do not have.

BREAKING NEWS

>> Some students are abusing drugs not to get high, but to try to help them do better in school. The prescription stimulants Ritalin and Adderall help those who have ADD/ADHD and related problems with concentration and focus. Students may fake

DRUGS ONLINE

Teens are also buying drugs through illegal online pharmacies. It's a highly dangerous way to get drugs. Buyers have no idea what they are really getting when the drugs arrive. The drugs may not even be those advertised by the site. Or the drugs may have a potency that is harmful to the user. Teens may also raid medicine cabinets of friends and neighbors to steal prescription pills that they know little about.

Teens can buy illegal drugs through online pharmacies.

No matter how illegal drugs are bought, one thing remains the same—buying and taking them is breaking the law. Taking a pill that has been prescribed to someone else is also illegal. Teens caught possessing or selling drugs can be arrested. And the legal consequences can be very serious. However, what drugs do inside the body can be much more serious.

symptoms in order to get a prescription from their doctor. They may also know someone at school who sells or has a prescription he or she is willing to share. These drugs have the same addictive qualities as cocaine and morphine. Very little is yet known about the long-term effects of these drugs.

The brain is the most complex organ in the human body. And once drugs are taken, that's where they head. Once drugs hit the brain they start changing the way it works. The brain then sends mixed signals to the body.

Drugs interfere with the way a person's brain works.

Drugs affect three areas of the brain. They include the brain stem, the limbic system, and the cerebral cortex. Each area controls different functions of the body, from the senses to feelings of pleasure to breathing. To control these functions, the brain sends messages from one area to another. These messages are sent through nerve cells. Chemicals extend from one cell to another, letting the messages travel through the brain.

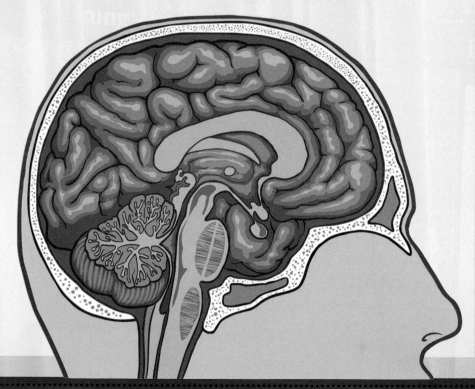

BREAKING NEWS

>> During puberty, the brain goes through some big changes. Research has shown that taking drugs during puberty may change how the brain grows.

SENDING MESSAGES

Some drugs mimic the chemicals that connect brain cells. Then they send abnormal messages throughout the brain. Marijuana and heroin are two drugs that do this. Other drugs interfere with the messages sent. They increase the chemicals sent between cells. This makes the messages have a much bigger impact than they normally would. Meth and cocaine do this to the brain.

The good feeling made by drugs is created by the release of dopamine in the brain. Dopamine is a chemical that controls emotion and pleasure. Drugs allow more dopamine to be released. The result of this is that the brain adjusts to the dopamine release so that when a person is not taking the drugs, it releases less dopamine than normal. This makes a person feel unhappy.

Once taken, drugs head straight to the brain.

Research also shows that addiction is a type of learning. If the brain learns to function on drugs, it makes it more likely that teen users will later become addicts.

The mixed messages sent from the brain during drug taking make the body do unusual things. Drugs affect the senses and functions of the body.

Certain drugs cause hallucinations. This is when a person sees or hears things that do not exist. Sometimes these things are really scary, such as people or monsters attacking the person. Or hallucinations can make impossible acts seem possible, such as being able to fly. Believing these hallucinations can cause people to do unsafe things. Sometimes people jump out of windows or off buildings. Users can also become violent, imagining that others are trying to hurt them.

Stimulants increase a person's energy. They can make a user feel anxious, talkative, and irritable. Stimulants also increase a person's heart rate and body temperature. Users lose their appetite when on the drug and can go without eating for a long time.

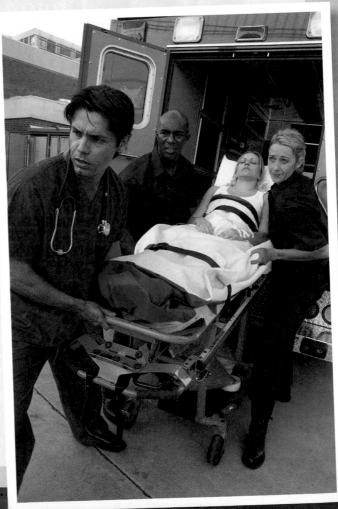

A drug overdose can cause serious health problems or even death.

SIDE EFFECTS

Different prescription drugs have different side effects. Blood pressure and heart rate are raised with Adderall. OxyContin causes drowsiness. And some people have really dangerous reactions to prescription drugs. They can go into a coma, have seizures, and, in some cases, even die.

Many times teens mix drugs. The effects combine and multiply. This can lead to dehydration, loss of coordination, and breathing and heart problems. It can cause teens to stay high for long periods of time—even for hours or days. Or drugs can lead teens straight to the emergency room.

UNDERCOVER STORY
DEADLY COMBINATION

Eighteen-year-old Joey Rovero did well in school and was a great athlete. However, he made a deadly decision on December 18, 2009. He was at a party with some friends. He drank alcohol and took two kinds of prescription medicine: Xanax and Oxycodone. He did not take a deadly amount of each drug, but the combined effects were more than his body could handle. The drugs slowed down Rovero's nervous system, he stopped breathing, and he died.

CHAPTER THREE

THE EFFECTS OF DRUGS

Megan had been sexually abused when she was younger. And she had no idea how to deal with her problems. She wanted to cover up the pain in her life and thought drugs might help. Megan was just 13 years old when she first tried drugs. First it was marijuana. Then she moved on to inhalants. Megan huffed anything she could find in the house.

Megan's parents thought something was wrong and sent Megan to counseling. She didn't listen to her parents or therapist. She just waited until she could get back to huffing. It was an escape from life for Megan. Her addiction soon grew out of control, and Megan was huffing whenever she could. She no longer cared if anyone discovered her drug use. Her parents did find out that

Casual drug use can lead to a daily addiction.

BREAKING NEWS

>> According to a report by CASAColumbia, "Adolescent Substance Use: America's #1 Public Health Problem," starting drug taking when young leads to higher risks of addiction.

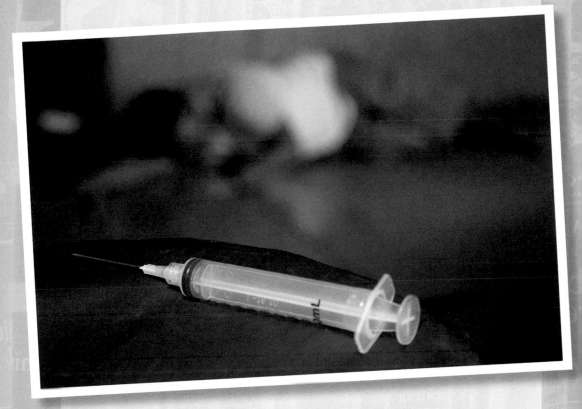

Addiction makes users not care about anything but getting and using drugs.

she had begun using again, and she was sent to rehab at 14. It was during treatment that Megan realized, "Huffing could have killed me. I started to huff when I was 13 years old...that's too young to do a lot of things, including becoming an addict, or dying."

ABUSING FROM AN EARLY AGE

Just like Megan, many people begin abusing drugs as teenagers. They may have a history of drug abuse in their families. They may be trying to cover up painful memories. Or teens may be trying to fit in with their friends. Drug use can start for many reasons. No matter how it starts, drug abuse will most likely lead to problems.

The study found that nine out of ten Americans who fit the medical category of addiction started smoking, drinking, or using drugs before they were 18.

At first, drug abuse is not noticeable. Teens take drugs when parents aren't around, and the effects wear off quickly. Or teens figure out really good ways to hide their drug use. They use excuses to explain their odd actions or moods. However, things quickly change as addiction takes over.

HARD TO HIDE

A habit is harder to hide when it the drug use occurs every day. And supporting a daily habit can be expensive. Teens don't usually have a lot of money available, so they find ways to get the money they need. They steal from family and friends or sell personal items to get cash. They take bigger risks, not caring about the social and legal consequences.

HITTING THE HEADLINES
FACES OF METH

The physical results of addiction can be very alarming. People change dramatically. It makes a big impact to see the physical toll drugs take on a person's body. The Faces of Meth program shows a series of mug shots of meth addicts. The first photo for each person is of an early arrest, while the second is of a later arrest. The differences are shocking. Later photos show people with sunken eyes and cheeks and scarred and scabbed faces. Meth mouth is also a disturbing result of meth addiction. Meth causes broken, discolored, and rotten teeth. Meth stops saliva production, which allows acids in the mouth to eat away at the teeth. Users also grind their teeth and forget to brush or floss. It leaves the teeth looking black and worn down.

With daily drug use comes a physical and emotional toll. These are the signs to watch for to know if someone has a drug problem:

- **Skipping out on responsibilities:** Missing classes and work, getting bad grades in school, and not doing chores at home.

- **Increased risk taking:** Driving under the influence, meeting up with strangers.

- **Legal trouble:** Getting arrested, stealing.

- **Emotional issues:** Fighting with family and friends, becoming more isolated from others, emotional highs and lows, anxiety and nervousness.

- **Physical signs:** Sudden weight loss, bloodshot eyes, changes in sleeping patterns, picking at the skin and sores.

Drugs change how a person acts and looks.

Taking drugs can lead to some serious social problems. With an altered mind comes poor judgment. Users take risks by driving cars while under the influence. On the road, they can kill themselves, passengers, and other drivers in car accidents.

DRUGS AND RISK TAKING

Teens who take drugs may be involved in violent situations. Under the influence of drugs, they put themselves in danger of being harmed by weapons or physical abuse. And teens on drugs take sexual risks as well. They may have unprotected sex resulting in a disease or pregnancy. They may also be photographed in the midst of risky behavior. These photos can make their way around social media, ruining a teen's reputation.

Using drugs leads to bad choices, sometimes resulting in unplanned pregnancies.

BREAKING NEWS

>> Researchers at Washington University School of Medicine found that pregnancies are linked with drug, tobacco, and alcohol use by teens. The study looked at 14,000 high school students.

DRUGS AND SCHOOL

If a teen chooses drugs over school, the negative consequences may endure for years. They could even change the teen's academic and professional future. Drug use can lead to failing grades and lower grade point averages. This can affect what college will accept that teen after graduation. Teens can be expelled if found using drugs at school. They then must find another way to finish school.

Drug use can end friendships, too. Users become isolated, spending a lot of time on their own. They stop answering phone calls and texts. Using becomes the most important thing in their lives. This can then lead to depression and loneliness. And the most extreme result of these feelings is suicide.

Studying and tests can become less important to someone abusing drugs.

These teens answered questions about drug and other substance use, sexual activity, and other risky behaviors. The results showed that students who smoked, drank, used drugs, or carried weapons to school were more likely to become pregnant or get another person pregnant.

Drugs also have long-term consequences. If caught buying or selling drugs, a teen can have lasting legal problems. Different states have different laws, but all have strict laws relating to drugs. If convicted of a drug-related offense, the impact on a teen's future can be great. He or she may not get the job applied for as an adult. He or she may not be able to join the military or receive college loans, and may even have to serve time in jail.

Many homeless teens have drug abuse problems.

A HISTORY OF ABUSE

Many young homeless teens have a history of drug abuse. They may become homeless because of their addiction or other reasons. If they didn't have a drug problem before living on the streets, they often develop one while on the streets. The National Network for Youth states that 40 to 50 percent of homeless youth have drug problems. They also found that homeless youth are more likely than other teens to try crack, marijuana, and other drugs.

HOMELESS AND HUNGRY PLEASE HELP

BREAKING NEWS

>> Homeless teens do not always become homeless because of addiction. However, living on the streets is stressful, scary, and often dangerous. It can lead to drug addiction and mental health issues.

Drugs can also make the body suffer long-term damage. Some effects are unknown, but are being tested. Some animal tests show that Ecstasy causes brain damage in animals. Inhalants break down a chemical in the brain. Over time this can cause tremors and muscle spasms. Inhalants can also cause heart and

Drug abuse can lead users to commit crimes and spend time in jail.

liver damage. Stimulants can cause mental issues, such as paranoia and delusions. They can also make people lose their teeth and become anorexic. Different drugs do different damage, but they all cause long-term and serious harm.

This, in turn, can result in risky behavior and increase the chance of unsafe sex. When dealing with the basic problems of finding food and shelter, it becomes even harder to kick a drug habit. It is a vicious cycle for homeless teens.

CHAPTER FOUR

GETTING HELP

Sam first tried meth with some of her high school friends. She liked it and began using regularly. It made Sam feel good, and it also made her lose weight. That felt great, since Sam had never liked her body. However, soon the meth was eating away at her life. Sam was fighting with her family. She was paranoid, too. She stayed in her room for days. And her weight really dropped—from 145 pounds (66 kg) to just 100 pounds (45 kg).

Fighting with family is a sign of drug abuse.

Sam started treatment nine months after she first tried meth. A few weeks later, Sam relapsed and used. She went on to relapse two more times. After being clean for 45 days, Sam was released from the rehab center. She started seeing a therapist and moved back in with her family. Sam knew staying sober wouldn't be easy, though. She had to go to her Narcotics Anonymous meetings and stay away from bad influences. Being sober would take work for the rest of Sam's life.

STEPS TOWARD RECOVERY

For addicts like Sam, detox and rehab centers are the first steps toward recovery. Getting off drugs is hard, but staying off them can be even harder. Most drug users relapse several times over many years. Each day is a constant battle to stay sober. But with the right support, former users can have happy lives without drugs.

UNDERCOVER STORY

WHY IS QUITTING SO HARD?

Drugs are hard to quit, and relapse is just a part of recovery. That's because addiction can be as much a mental condition as a physical one. Some people are ordered to go to treatment by the court or they are pressured by friends and family to go. They may not want to quit. Treatment can help a person stop using—but treatment is not a cure for addiction.

Getting help is the first step to stopping drug abuse. Help may be offered by friends and family. They stage an intervention with the user. An intervention is when friends or family confront someone who has an addiction problem. They offer their support to help get the teen off drugs.

PHYSICAL AND MENTAL

Drug addiction is both a physical and mental problem. To get rid of the physical addiction, the body needs to release all of the drugs in its system. This is called detoxification, or detox. This process is done at a detox center. During detox, a person can experience terrible withdrawal symptoms, depending on the drug. Some of these symptoms include sweating, nausea, and hallucinations. The symptoms are the result of the body getting the drugs out if its system. Doctors help the person safely get rid of the drugs at the center.

A friend's support can help save a drug user's life.

HITTING THE HEADLINES

GROUP THERAPY: A BAD INFLUENCE?

Sometimes rehab can be harmful, not helpful. A recent *Time* magazine article claimed that group therapy can be a bad influence for teens. The teens hear stories about drug use and may then want to try the drugs mentioned. "Many programs throw casual dabblers together with hard-core addicts . . . Just putting kids in group therapy actually promotes greater drug use," said Dr. Nora Volkow, director of the National Institute on Drug Abuse.

FINDING TREATMENT

After detox, the next step is a treatment center. This is a center with doctors, therapists, and other drug users seeking recovery. The treatment can include therapy, which is talking about a person's problems. It helps a user understand why he or she started using.

The person may have a problem that has never been resolved. Therapy can help the person deal with that problem. Medications can help a person deal with mental health issues or remaining physical problems. Treatment can take a few weeks to several months. The length of treatment depends on the person's level of addiction.

Returning to normal life can be hard for someone just out of treatment. Old friends may be around. Bad influences can tempt a teen to use again. It's easy to fall back into bad habits. It's much harder to stay clean.

Having support helps former drug users stay clean.

Support groups help teens stay off drugs. These groups meet regularly. They are places where former addicts can discuss their temptations with people who will not judge them. Some support groups are just for teens. In these groups, teens meet others experiencing the same challenges. It helps teens know that they are not alone in their fight to stay clean.

BREAKING NEWS

>> Relapse is common. Here are the facts on treatment and relapsing:

• Around 40 to 60 percent of people relapse after being in treatment.

Stress is a common risk factor for a drug relapse.

STUMBLING BLOCKS

Despite having the support of others, relapse can happen to anyone. And it usually happens a few times during recovery. Certain things can trigger a relapse, such as stress and being around others using drugs. Boredom, isolation, and mental or physical illness are other common triggers. Teens must know their triggers and do their best to stay away from them. That is the best way to prevent relapses. After a relapse, teens usually go back to a treatment center.

- Longer treatment may lessen the number of relapses an addict has. The National Institute on Drug Abuse found that cocaine users who were in treatment for less than 90 days were more likely to have relapses. Thirty-five percent relapsed, while only 17 percent of those treated for 90 days or more relapsed.

CHAPTER FIVE

SOCIETY AND DRUGS

Many drugs are illegal in the United States. These illegal drugs are mostly used to get high. However, some drugs are used in different cultures for religious reasons. And marijuana is used in some states for medical purposes.

Indian hemp is used in India and Africa for religious ceremonies. Some mushrooms cause hallucinations. They are used in Latin America by native peoples. And native peoples of Mexico use peyote for religious purposes.

In some states, people with a prescription can buy medical marijuana at certain pharmacies.

BREAKING NEWS

>> A whole industry has grown up around medical marijuana. In Colorado, businesses now specialize in making products containing medical marijuana. These include lemon bars, sodas, and candies.

USES OF DRUGS

Peyote is part of a cactus, which when taken causes visions. Another drug used in South America is believed to heal its users. It is made from the stem bark of certain vines. These drugs are used to enhance religious experiences in different cultures. While these drugs are used ceremonially in these cultures, it does not mean they are safe. They have the potential to harm a person's mind and body. This is especially true if drugs are abused.

In some states, medical marijuana can be prescribed for anxiety, nausea, anorexia, or other health issues.

Marijuana is a plant that is smoked or eaten. It is thought to relieve pain, anxiety, nausea, anorexia, some eye problems, and seizures. In 2013, in the United States, 17 states allowed the use of medical marijuana. The patient must have a prescription for medical marijuana for its use to be legal. Making medical marijuana legal in other states is a hotly debated issue.

This industry makes a lot of money selling marijuana products to people with medical conditions. However, some people think that patients may not have true medical conditions. In Colorado, 94 percent of people with prescriptions had them for "severe pain." This symptom is very difficult to measure or prove.

Schools are one of the most common places where teens buy and sell drugs. Some schools have begun randomly drug testing their students to combat the problem. They also select students who they believe may be using drugs and and ask them to provide a sample of their urine to be tested.

Schools want to decrease drug use among students. If a student tests positive, interventions and treatment may be recommended to the student and his or her family. Early intervention is vital to preventing later drug addiction. Students can also be expelled from school for using drugs.

HITTING THE HEADLINES

CHALLENGING DRUG LAWS

The American Civil Liberties Union (ACLU) takes on cases that challenge laws affecting civil rights. In Pennsylvania, the ACLU and some parents sued two school districts in 2011. They believed the drug testing policy in these districts was not constitutional. Daughters of the parents would not sign the form allowing mandatory initial drug testing and later random drug testing. Because of this, the girls were not allowed to participate in sports or other activities. A Pennsylvania Supreme Court judge later ruled that the school's drug testing policy was unconstitutional. The school had no evidence that there was a drug problem at the school. The judge believed the drug testing was not justified.

STUDENT RIGHTS

Drug testing can be seen as an invasion of students' rights. School districts have been challenged for enforcing random drug testing at schools in Pennsylvania, Texas, and Washington. However, the U.S. Supreme Court ruled in June 2002 that public schools could randomly drug test students participating in extracurricular activities like athletes.

Little research has been carried out into whether drug testing works in schools. And the tests are not 100 percent accurate. The drug tests are also given only to students who participate in sports or drive to school. However, some people believe that this testing is helpful because it deters students from ever trying drugs.

Most students don't take drugs at school.

Prevention is important in reducing drug abuse amongst teens. And the media is a powerful tool for educating teens on the dangers of drug use.

The National Institute on Drug Abuse (NIDA) has a Web site for teens about the science behind drug use and abuse. Teens can learn what different drugs do to the brain and the body. They can also find out the long-term effects of different drugs. Learning about the science of drugs takes the mystery out of drug use. Teens sometimes think that nothing can hurt them. However, science shows that drugs can do serious damage.

By discussing their effects, students learn just how much drugs can hurt them.

HITTING THE HEADLINES
EDUCATING TEENS

National Drug Facts Week is a media campaign that aims to teach teens about drugs and drug abuse. It is held at the end of January each year. During the week, community events are held. NIDA provides toolkits so that schools can hold their own conversations about drugs. Students can also ask NIDA scientists questions about drugs and their effects.

FACING UP TO DRUGS

The Just Think Twice Web site was created by the Drug Enforcement Agency (DEA). It outlines the real consequences of different drug-related situations. It also shares the facts and myths about drug use.

The Drug Abuse Resistance Education (D.A.R.E.) program is taught in 75 percent of American school districts. Police officers teach students how to resist peer pressure and stay drug-free.

There are many other local and state programs designed to educate teens about drugs. It is also important for parents to talk with teens about the consequences of using drugs. They may not even be aware of the health problems drugs cause or the risk of addiction. Parents can be the best help for teens at risk of becoming addicts.

If teens grow up to be adult addicts, the cost can be high for society. These costs include increased criminal activity. Adults with severe, drug-related mental health issues can negatively affect communities. Children also pay the price for their parents' addictions. Babies can be born addicted to drugs or with defects as a result of their mothers' drug use.

Babies can suffer from the drugs used by their mothers during pregnancy.

CRIMINALS AND DRUGS

Drugs and crime are linked. Offenders fill jails and, while there, use drugs as well. The U.S. Department of Justice reports that almost half of the people in jail are there because of drug offenses.

Trafficking drugs is also a huge international problem. Drug trafficking is the trade of illegal drugs around the world. Once drugs make it to the United States, gangs take over. They control the distribution of illegal drugs.

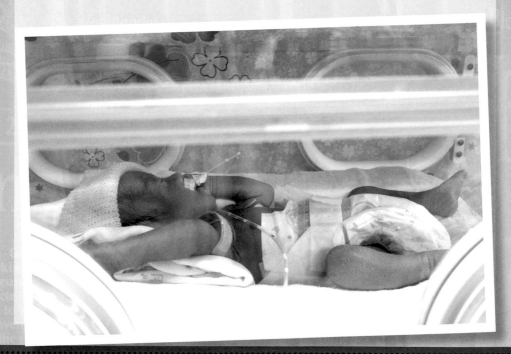

BREAKING NEWS

>> The financial cost to society as a result of drug abuse is significant. A recent CASAColumbia report found that substance abuse and addiction cost local, state, and federal governments $467.7 billion

Jail time can be the consequence of illegal drug sales, purchases, and use.

GANG WARFARE

Gangs use violence to resolve their issues with other gangs. This leads to deadly shootings that kill gang members and also innocent people caught in the crossfire.

Over time, drug addiction can also make mental health issues worse. Drug addicts with mental illnesses can be very difficult to treat. They may be hard to deal with, losing the support of families or groups. They may relapse often and need to be hospitalized.

Drug addiction can affect helpless victims. Babies born to addicts suffer from the same addictions as their mothers. Drugs can also cause birth defects in babies. They can be born before they are due, be underweight, or even die in the womb. These babies may also have severely damaged brains.

Drug addiction takes a toll on many people other than the addict and can cause problems throughout society.

in one year. The study found that most of the money was spent on health care, while $47 billion was spent on justice systems.

DRUGS—THE TRUTH

The truth about drugs is that they affect many teens and can have devastating effects. Drugs may seem to be a way to escape life, but science shows that drugs just send mixed messages from the brain to the rest of the body.

The teen brain is still developing and can be permanently harmed by drug abuse. Drugs also have effects that make teens engage in risky behavior, which can have terrible consequences. Once addiction takes over, the effects can cause permanent damage.

Without drugs, teens can live healthy lives.

HOPE FOR THE FUTURE

There is help for teens who abuse drugs, however. Treatment centers and support groups provide ways for teens to stop using and stay clean. Prevention is also very important. Learning about the effects of drugs may be all that a teen needs to know to avoid drugs. Parents, teachers, friends, and counselors can provide support and advice for teens using or at risk of using drugs. And media can be an important tool, showing users what happens to the body and mind from drug abuse.

The teen years are a crucial time to learn about the effects of drugs. Teen users have a high risk of becoming adult addicts. Education and early intervention can stop that from happening.

UNDERCOVER STORY

FROM DRUG ABUSER TO BEAUTY QUEEN

Nicole Hansen was 17 when she first started using Ecstasy at raves. Then she moved on to cocaine, mushrooms, and other drugs. She overdosed and almost died one night. However, she survived and decided to stop using. She quit drugs and eventually got her life back on track with the support of her family. She entered the Miss Teen Utah beauty contest in 2001. Other contestants thought she shouldn't be allowed to enter because of her drug past. She proved them wrong. She knew she deserved to be there and won the contest. Anyone can fall into abusing drugs, but, with support, recovery is possible too.

GLOSSARY

abnormal Not normal; unusual.

addiction When the body and mind crave and depend on particular substances, such as food, drugs, or alcohol.

confidence A feeling or awareness of one's own power.

consequence The result of a cause or action.

constitutional Adhering to the laws of a country that balance the rights of its people with the powers of the government.

dehydration Not having enough water in a person's body.

depression A mental illness that causes severe sadness.

dopamine A chemical in the brain that controls pleasure.

hallucinations Seeing things in the mind that do not really exist.

hormones Chemicals made in the body that affect how a person grows and develops.

intervention An action taken to improve or change a situation.

paranoia Often irrational or unfounded feelings of mistrust and suspicion.

potency How strong or powerful something is.

prescription An order for drugs written by a doctor to a pharmacist on behalf of a patient.

synthetic Something that is made, rather than found in nature.

tolerance The lessening of a body's response to a drug.

tremors Shaking or trembling movements of the hands, arms, or legs.

voluntary Willing to, not forced to, do something.

FOR MORE INFORMATION

BOOKS

Cross, Carrie L. *Crystal Meth*. New York, NY: Crabtree Publishing, 2011.

Edelfield, Bruce, and Tracey J. Moosa. *Drug Abuse*. New York, NY: Rosen Publishing, 2011.

Field, Jon Eben. *Inhalants and Solvents*. New York, NY: Crabtree Publishing, 2011.

Freedman, Jeri. *Your Beautiful Brain: Keeping Your Brain Healthy*. New York, NY: Rosen Central, 2012.

Kimlan, Lanie, and Anne Alvergue. *The Truth About Ecstasy*. New York, NY: Rosen Publishing, 2011.

Marsico, Katie. *Heroin*. New York, NY: Marshall Cavendish, 2014.

Spilsbury, Louise. *Harmful Substances*. New York, NY: PowerKids Press, 2011.

ORGANIZATIONS

Teen Line
P.O. Box 48750
Los Angeles, CA 90048
(310) 855-HOPE (4673) or (800) TLC-TEEN (852-8336)
Web site: http://teenlineonline.org
A site and phone line run for teens by teens that deals with a variety of issues that affect young people.

WEB SITES

Due to the changing nature of Internet links, Rosen Publishing has developed an online list of Web sites related to the subject of this book. This site is updated regularly. Please use this link to access the list:

http://www.rosenlinks.com/UCS/Drug

INDEX